This Is as Bad as It Gets

Le Grand Tourbillon de la Vie, Le Pire N'est Même pas Certain, and L'amour Triomphe Toujours
first published in France © 1997, 1998, and 2000 by Le Cherche-Midi Editeur.

07 08 09 10 11 WKT 10 9 8 7 6 5 4 3 2 1

ISBN-13: 978-0-7407-4672-7
ISBN-10: 0-7407-4672-3
Library of Congress Control Number: 2004111633

www.andrewsmcmeel.com

Voutch

This Is as Bad as It Gets

« A Voutch Cartoon »
Collection

**Andrews McMeel
Publishing, LLC**

Kansas City

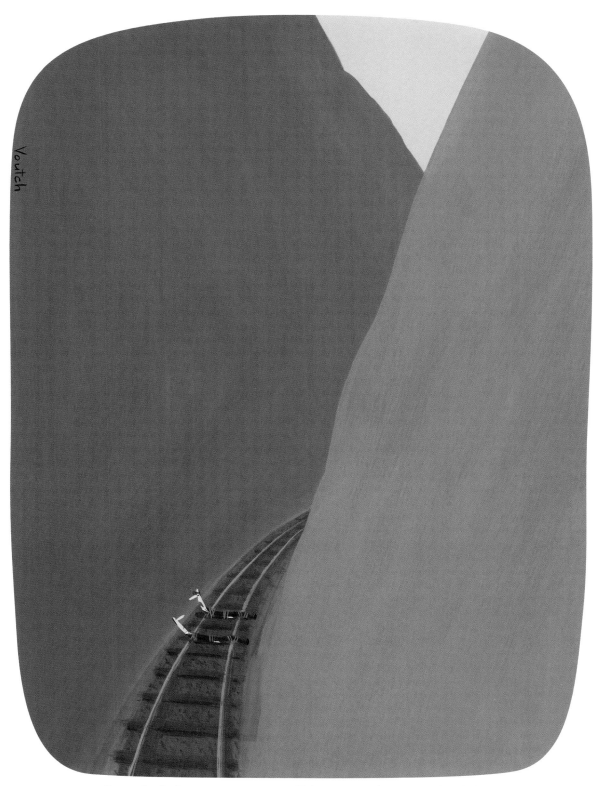

You are beginning to get on my nerves, Maloney, you and your eternal optimism.

Gotta go now, I have to charge the net.

O Almighty, reduce my enemies to dust. As well as some of my friends. I have too many.

Good morning, Natalya. What is my diabolical plan for the day?

As your leader, I will be harsh but fair. To be perfectly
honest, I will be much more harsh than fair.

We have no ideas. *You* have no ideas. And *together,* we will win this fight!

The city council has decided to post signs on each public beach at the beginning of the season with the warning "No Swimming—Highly Radioactive." However, at the request of the tourism industry professionals, these signs will be printed in Old Bulgarian and the skull and crossbones, deemed too alarming, will be replaced by a pretty little goldfish.

No, dear, that's not a clam, it's an old Nike.

It mostly reminds me that I forgot to buy toilet bowl cleanser again.

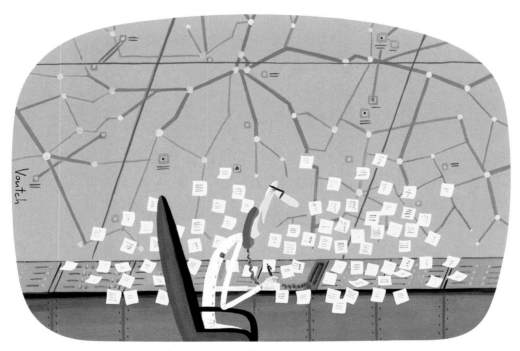

A huge radioactive leak at Reactor B-12?
Don't worry, I've made a note of it.

The onboard computer says that the onboard computer is about to crash.

News flash. We have just been informed that an airliner with 253 passengers
on board is currently crashing into downtown Grandville, causing many fatalities, including
Mr. Andrew Leonard, age thirty-four, who was eating his breakfast
cereal when the accident occurred.

Cyberflowers! They're wonderful!
Oh, Peter, you shouldn't have!

My darling, how wonderful it is to be able to communicate with you so easily. The immensity of I on the other; I speak, you respond, you speak and I respond, what an extraordinary revolution! class, language, culture, religion, or color. Which reminds me, I'm missing a purple sock.

the seas, the mountains, the plains that separate us no longer exist. You on one side of the planet,
This is super-communication. Individuals expressing themselves, interacting freely, regardless of country,
It's not in my suitcase. Could you check to see if it's in the laundry hamper?

Good old Mother Nature. Not only do I like Melinda, but *you* seem,
my dear Xaviers 2 and 3, to be getting along just fine with her little clonettes.

And *exactly* the same thing for my clone.

I'm going to the market. If Bill Gates or Ben Bernanke calls,
just say, "He who laughs last, laughs best," then hang up.

Not big enough. We're basically looking for a garden that will allow us to laugh
out loud in the garden all summer long without bothering the neighbors.

Objection, Your Honor. With his unfounded, libelous testimony,
the witness is obviously trying to tarnish the image of the Mafia.

Our New York offices have closed. You can now write to us at the following address:
Rainy Day Pension Fund, Retirement Benefits Department, General Delivery, Bahamas.

It's really annoying. Every time I find something I like,
it's just too small for the house.

Call for you. It's the neighbor. He says he has
something very important to say about your sausages.

I'm warning you. I'm writing a tell-all book: names, places, dates, everything.

We have decided not to reprint *250 Delicious Salt Cod Recipes* because, quite simply, salt cod is so passé.

No, I'm not afraid of lions. And do you want to know why? I *am* a lion.

I once ate a mouse. It was *dis-gusting*.

OVENS
VIDEO
TV
VIDEO
AUDIO
Youtch

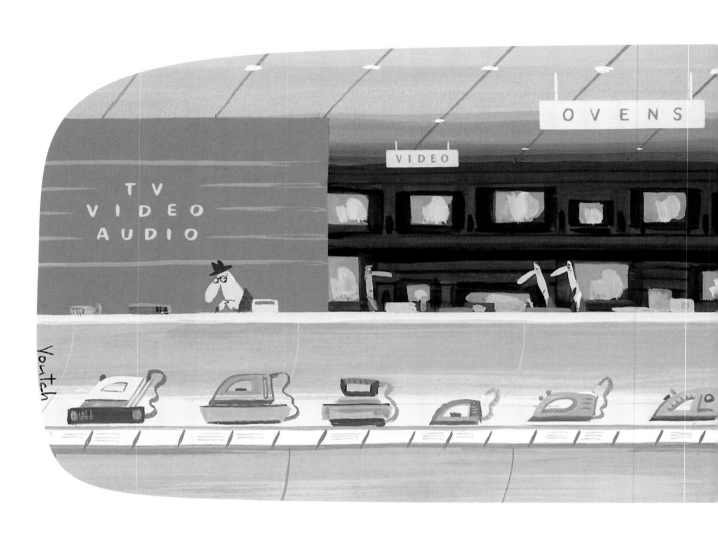

The digital iron? It's like a regular iron, only digital.

For the last time, Samantha, if you have something to tell me,
I'd rather you went through your lawyer.

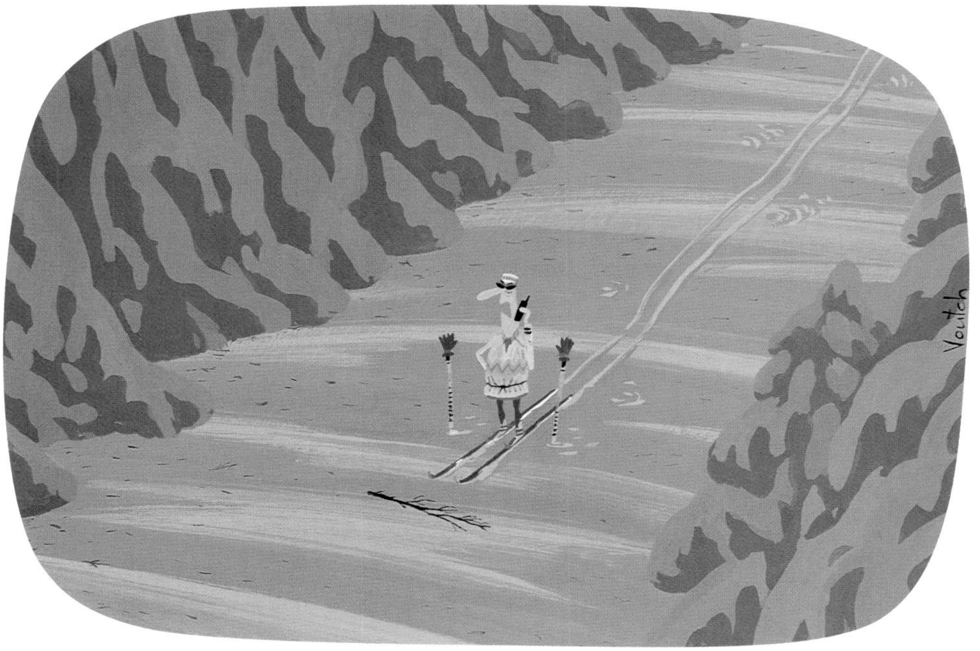
Voutch

Get me my lawyer.

May I have your attention please, may I have your attention please!
The store will be closing in three minutes!

I was closest. I guessed 1644 and the correct answer is 1944.

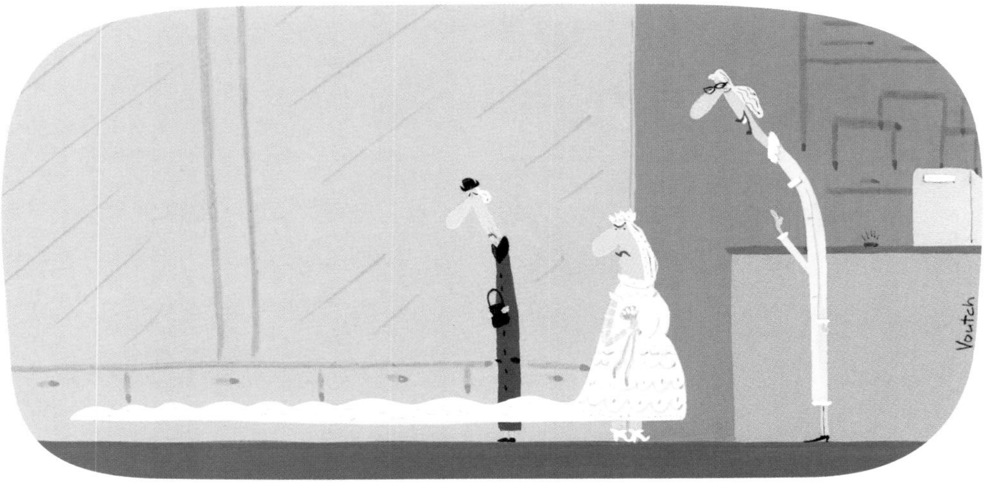
Voutch

Starched, articulated lace in polyester Kevlar imitation raw silk.
Either you like it or you don't. Generally, you don't.

The "Succulent Wild Boar Corsican Style"?
It's a pork chop with noodles and a little ketchup.

I represent a major company that specializes in door-to-door sales of things
that people do not own. So naturally my first question is: What don't you own?

Are these two done, sweetie? I need to go out
and buy some bread and a little lettuce.

I absolutely *adore* it, I mean, all this *wildatudeness*.

Oh, great. Now *I'm* beginning to think it smells like plutonium, too.

Back in '74, I had a flash of lucidity. Since then, nothing.

Hey, you jobless losers, how's it going?

THEATER 2
THEATER 3
Vonatch

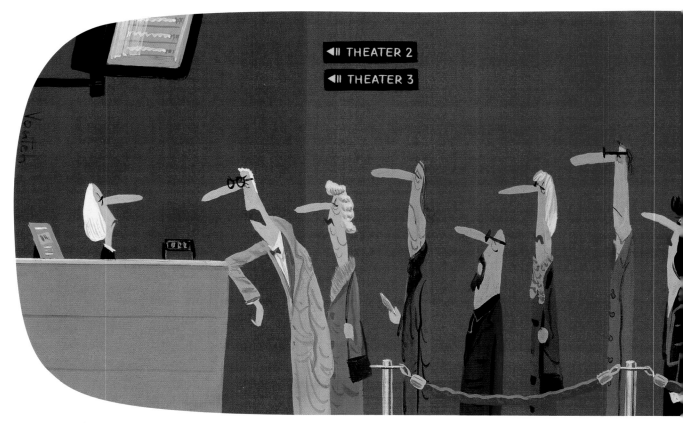

Personally, I like a good knee-slapper. My wife really doesn't.
So ideally you'll find us something in-between.

There is a gentleman outside who wants to know if you'd like to be his friend.

Our vacation is ruined. Even if it isn't
our upstairs neighbor, it looks so much like
him that the effect is exactly the same.

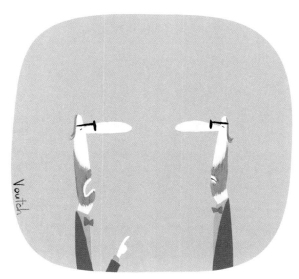

And stop calling me "clone."
You are the clone and I am *me*.

It's really getting on my nerves, Daphne. Why does *your* creativity
always have to take the same form as *my* creativity?

What? This is *scandalous!* *Absolutely shameful!* *Totally unacceptable!*
What do you mean, the "Learning to Cope" workshop is already *completely booked*?!?

The special issue of *Procrastinators Weekly*
from three weeks ago? No, we're sold out.

So I started a profound examination of myself and today, nearly fifteen years later,
I can say that the results are in. I no longer hate myself. I *despise* myself.

I'm afraid you don't understand. I do not *feel* completely lost in a cold
and hostile environment. I *am* completely lost in a cold and hostile environment.

I'd describe myself as someone who, in the course of his life,
has suffered 7,391 enormous disappointments.

And so one day I decided to spend more time with Lucille and the kids
and less time on long-range, laser-guided thermonuclear warheads.

Well, here comes your father the idiot,
late with the child support again.

We've managed to isolate your selfishness gene. It's huge.

And now, Doctor,
I want the truth.
Am I *really* insane?

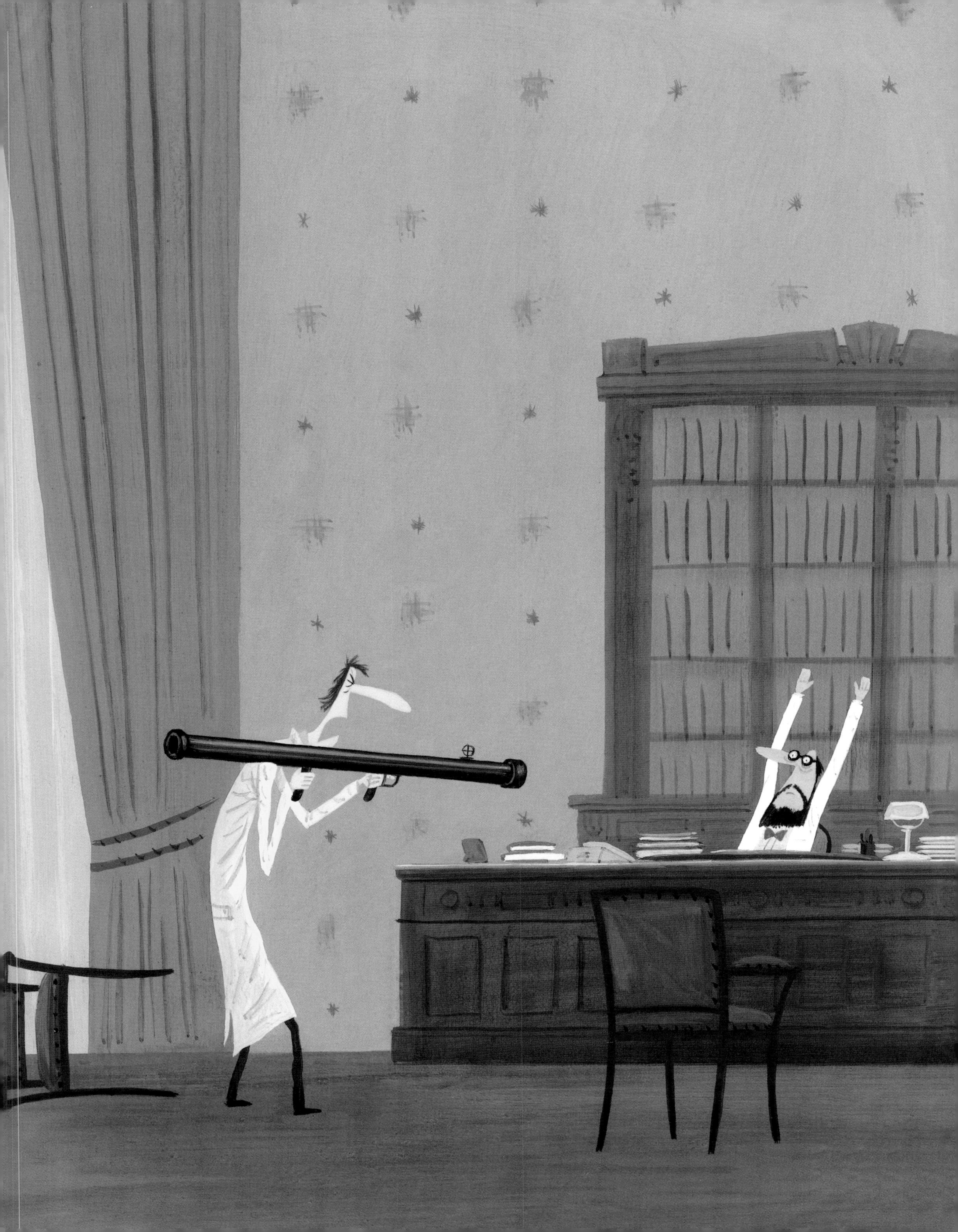

But of course, you're absolutely right; your mother
was never a showgirl in a seedy bar in Buenos Aires.
I confused your file with Mr. Dos Santos's.

As far as I am concerned, your psychoanalysis is over. I'm opening a pizzeria.

I did indeed say that I would adopt a homeless person. But remember
one thing: That evening I had three magnums of Château Pétrus '47.

There are only two things that are important in life, Marcello: Always love
your mother and never, ever, believe what the shrinks tell you.

My personal coach thinks you're a charlatan.

The three-day workshop will be moderated by the
celebrated Danish napologist Jan-Olaf Knutssen.

He's obviously trying to tell us something, but *what*?

I might have been able to perform a lifesaving operation on the 24th.
Unfortunately, on the 24th I will be skiing in St. Moritz.

Imagine for a moment that mankind forms an immense army marching
toward death. After reading your latest test results, let's just say that you are
simply going far ahead, like a scout.

We're off to a great start.
We have to rent the wings.

Can I call you back a little later?
I'm with a future widow and her husband.

All I can tell you today is this: You are suffering from egbertosis, a completely new disease, discovered on November 27, 2006—in other words, *today*—by Dr. Egbert—in other words, *me.*

I've made out my will. You inherit my genes and nothing else.

I took a look at your X-ray and thought,
"Well, there goes another customer."

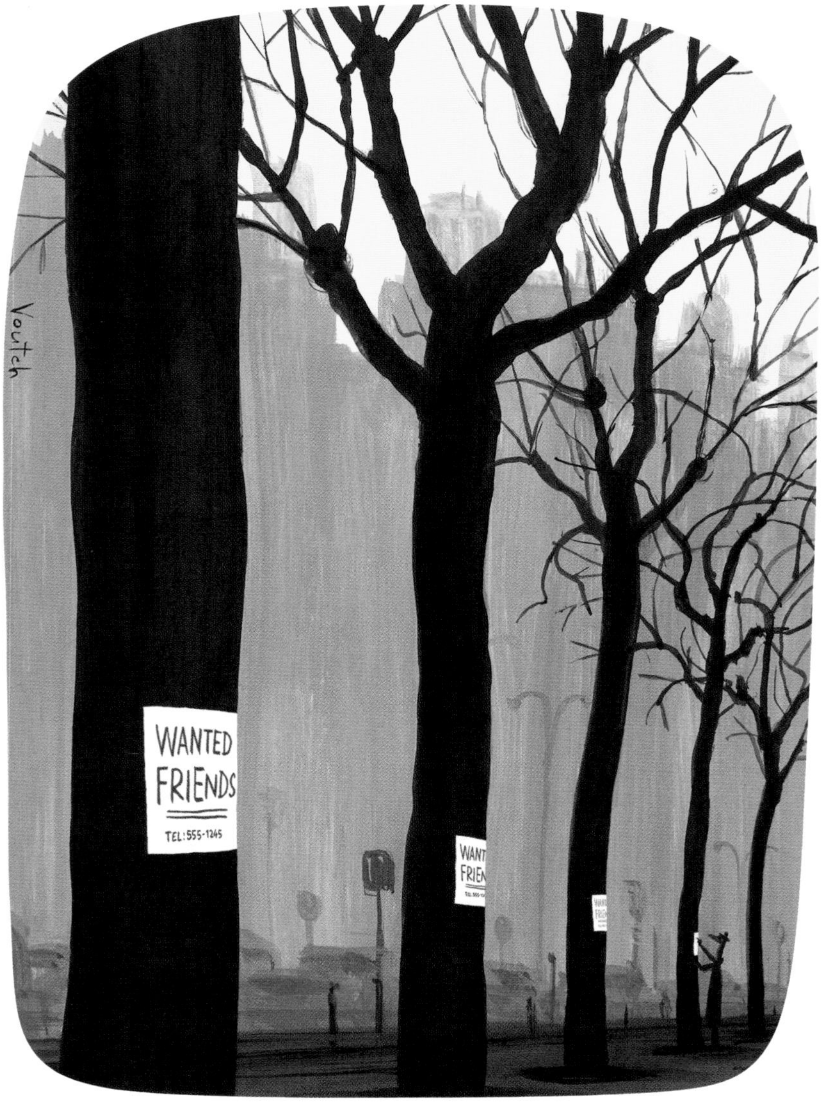
Voutch
WANTED
FRIENDS
TEL: 555-1245

Try to get it through your thick skull,
you stubborn mutt: I'm an individualist.

Let's be enemies, Martha. I would *so* like to share my self-hatred with you.

It so happens, Agnes, that I have met someone who makes a dark chocolate almond hazelnut fondant that is slightly superior to yours. So I am leaving you.

You know nothing about my problems as a woman! You know nothing about
women! You understand nothing about women! You're not even a woman!

Michael always treated me as an equal. But it didn't work.
It was always too much or not enough.

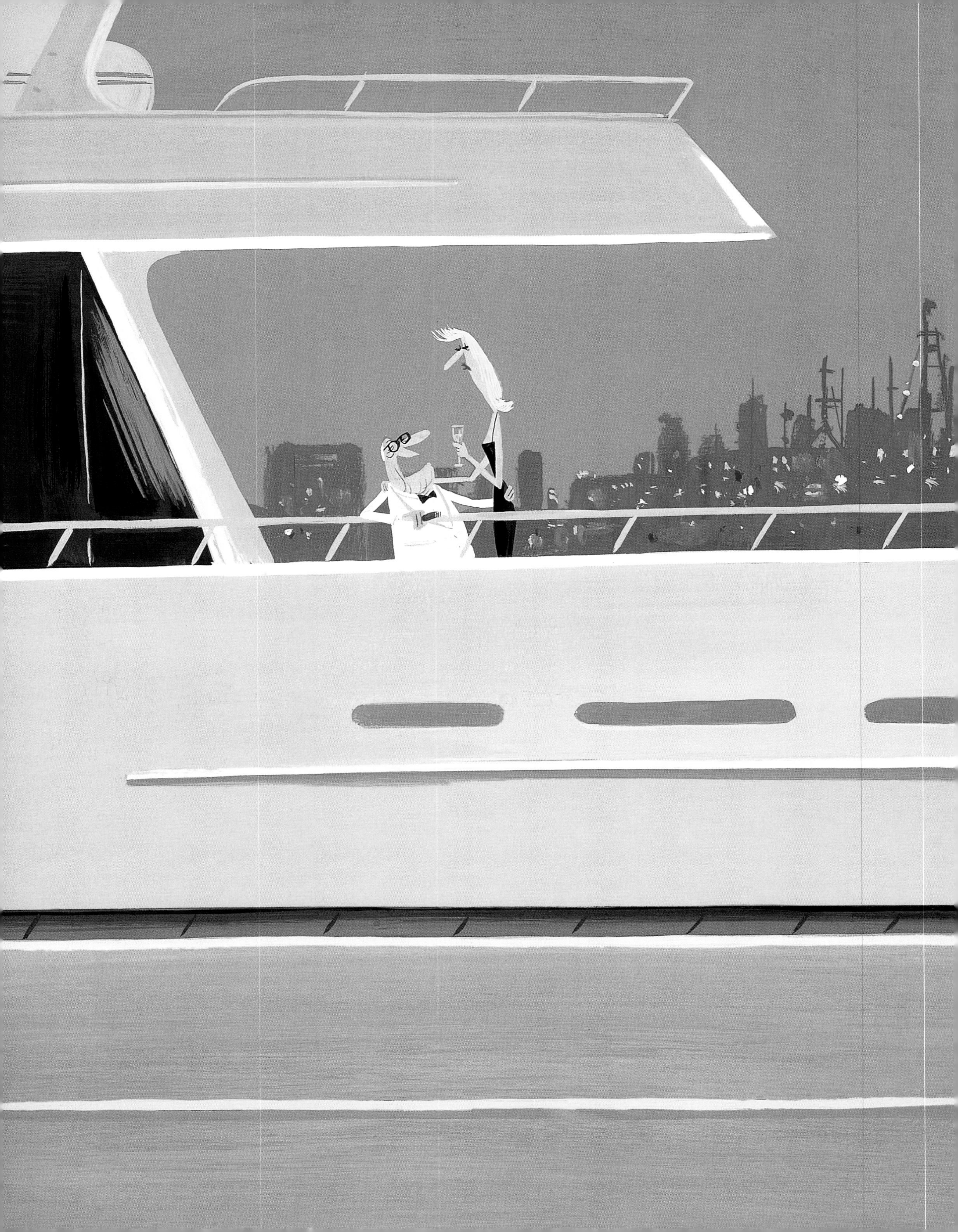

But, my sweet,
of course money always
serves a purpose.
You are *here*.

I dropped my glasses. A man picked them up. Our fingers touched.
I smelled his scent and suddenly my heart beat faster. And I thought: *He's the one.*
Then I put my glasses back on and I thought: *Maybe not.*

And the other problem, my love, is that you, too, are a male.

Let's just say I was expecting something much, much better.

Pleased to meet you.
I am Chauncey Boatwright IV,
but my friends all call me
Dom: *D*irty *O*ld *M*an.

OK, Venice it is. But I'm warning you: It's far.

Come on, Clarissa, think about it. We cannot relate as man and woman.
At best, we can relate as seagull to seagull.

Is this the first time you've gone pillaging?

Are you one of the following people:
Crawford, Cindy; Schiffer, Claudia; Campbell, Naomi?

No, Gertrude, sending two contract killers to my office is not
exactly what I would call initiating a constructive dialogue.

Six months ago, when I came up with this crazy idea of bringing all my exes
together for my birthday, I never for a moment thought you'd all be here with
me tonight. And I was right. Many couldn't make it.

It's me. I was just calling to tell you that there is a big white cloud coming.

If I were to cheat on you one day, you wouldn't get hurt. Because I'd make sure that you never knew, never doubted, never suspected. Like the day before yesterday, for example.

But *if* you were, would you tend to be more
A) sadistic; B) masochistic; or C) half and half?

Stop your sexual harassment, Bertha. Use a different
chat room and, while you're at it, use a different screen
name, too. Electrolux Queen is really too obvious.
I recognized you immediately.

To conclude, I would like to say that I have never believed in the

Internet, and recent events have clearly demonstrated one thing: I was wrong.

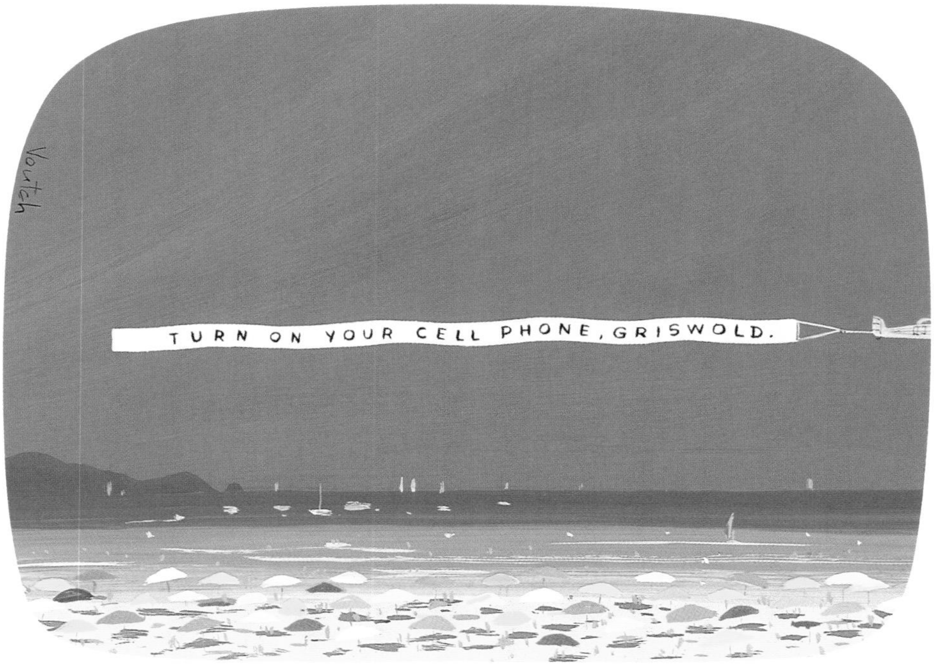
TURN ON YOUR CELL PHONE, GRISWOLD.
Voutch

That's what sets us apart, Beamish. You don't know how to say no, and I do.
Take your raise, for example. The answer is no.

Don't try to deny it, Wilson. We said "round," and Mr. Trumbull even added "round like a ball."

I have a problem, Beverly. Find a solution
right away and bring it to my office.

My wife would like to know
if you have any intention of giving
me a promotion, and if so, when.

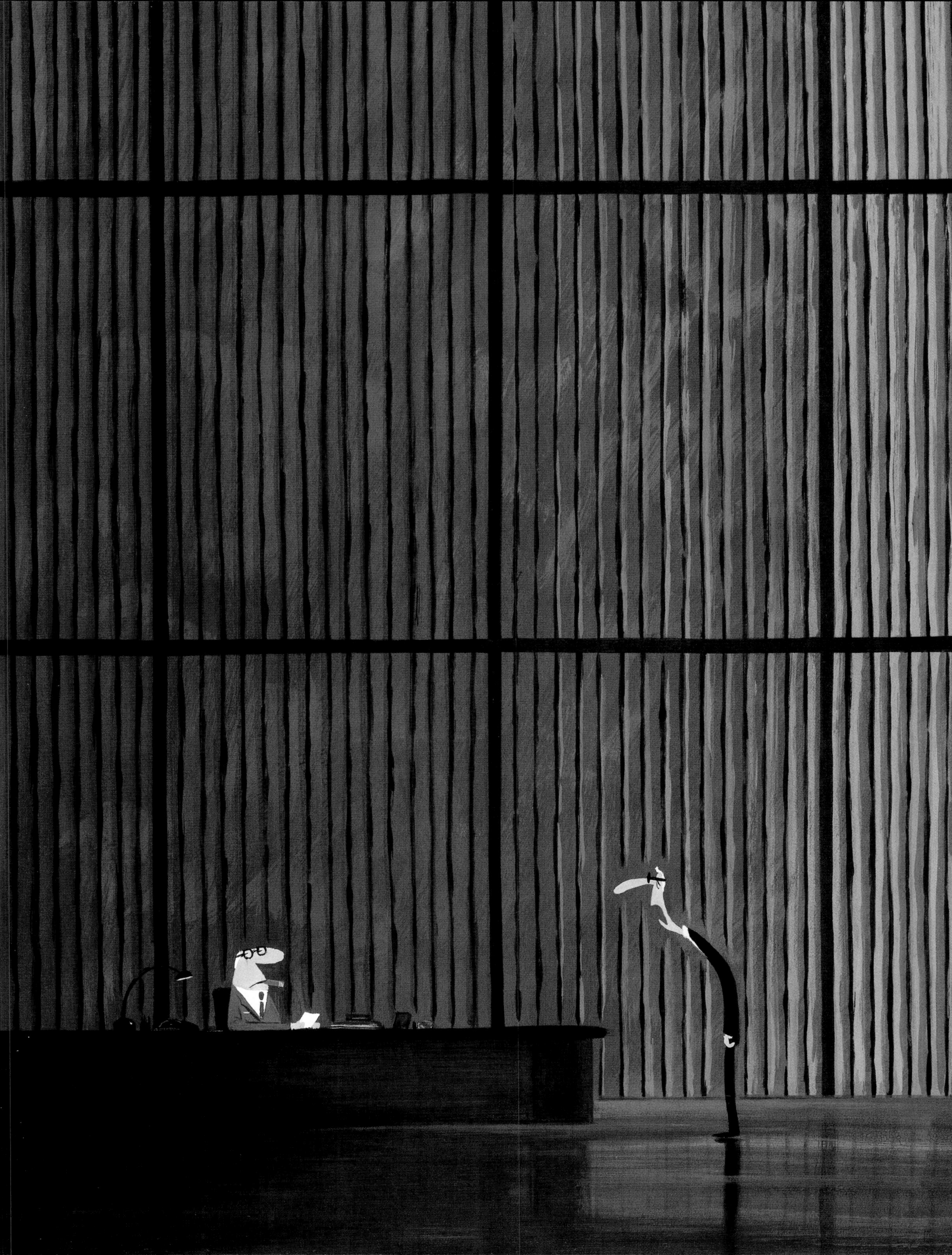

Tell everyone that I'm canceling the meeting on December 25 at 7:15 a.m.
I've just been informed of a religious holiday that falls on that date.

Mr. Superman is currently on sick leave.
I am his replacement, Mr. Gonzales.

I get it, I get it. You want to meet the leader of this planet, but which one?
The Great Bloot or the Little Sponks?

So Proposition A: "Row as hard as
we can against the current before it's
too late," wins by four votes to one,
with one abstention.

The good news is that the markets love the idea of downsizing: Gordon

EuroSteel-Unimetal has reversed its trend and was up 0.0648 points at closing.

I'll call you back. I'd like to discuss the matter with my associates:
Mr. Keyboard, Mr. Monitor, Ms. Printer, and Mr. Drawer.

Sherwood, all I'm saying is that this is not
what I'd call an appropriate managerial attitude.

Come on, Cosgrove, look on the bright side. Think of all the people
who'll be glad to hear you're back on the job market.

There's no changing my mind, Fenton. This time I've lost faith in you for good.

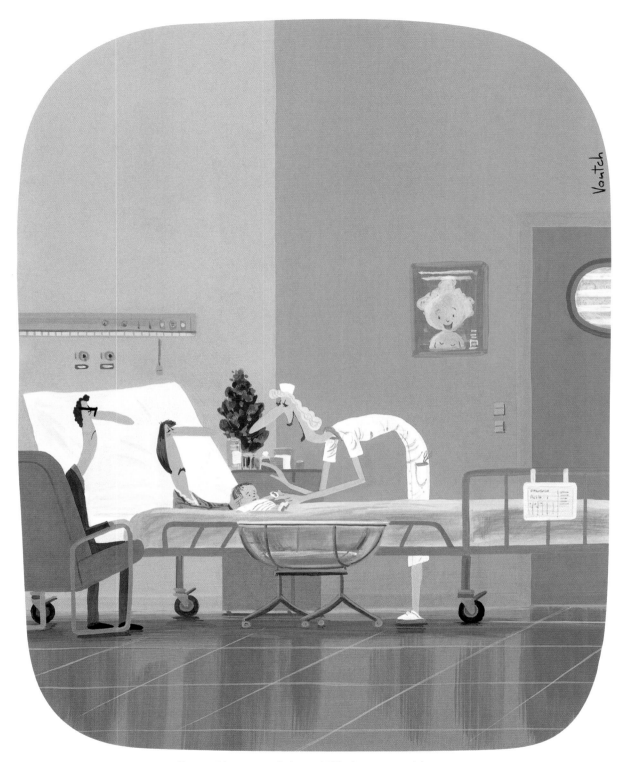

You say it's not your baby, and I'll take your word for it.
The intern in charge of the bracelets is really hopeless.

An exceptional destiny, Sire. He will be king
at the age of twenty-four. Then, at thirty-five, he will
have an operation and become queen.

I'm warning you, Jonathan. If your father comes home one day,
you are going to be in big, big trouble.

I am fully aware that your son's name
is Jason. But I am his nanny and I have
decided to call him Roberto. It's nicer,
right, my little Roberto?

Cecilia, does this mean that you've chosen not to make our separation
a moment of respect and dignity—a lasting monument to the exceptional
relationship we've had as man and wife?

I have stepdads all figured out. When there's one I don't like, I tell Mom that he gets a *really* weird look in his eyes when I put on my swimsuit, and pffft!—he's history.

Don't use that tone of voice with me. Do I have to remind you that *I'll* be the one who picks your retirement home?

And suddenly, I learned the truth. As you get older,
you don't get wiser. You get *older.*

There's nothing on TV. I'm going clubbing.

Granddad is out playing squash, Granny is at her Thai boxing
match, Grandma is hang gliding in the Rockies, Grandpa is training
for his triathlon, Mom and Dad are playing tennis, and I am
watching *Laguna Beach* and eating Snackens.

Stop calling me Great-Grandpa. It's so old-fashioned.
Call me *Bob*, like everybody else.

Your cousin Robert e-mailed to find out
if you were feeling better. I said no.